# Faith
## For
## Tough
## Times

## Robert H. Schuller

Thomas Nelson Publishers
*Nashville · Camden · New York*

Anything is possible
with faith

Jesus said to them, . . .
"for assuredly I say to you,
if you have faith as a mustard seed,
you will say to this mountain,
'Move from here to there,'
and it will move; and nothing
will be impossible for you."

MATTHEW 17:20

# Mountain Moving Power

$P$atty Wilson was thirteen years of age when it was discovered she was epileptic. Her dad knew she would encounter discrimination, that there would be those who would not hire her because she was epileptic. He knew he had to communicate to her that she too could react positively to her problem and that her life would be an inspiration to others.

Patty's father vowed to teach her that she could be supersuccessful. Just because she was epileptic didn't mean she had to be handicapped. He was going to make her believe in herself. She became interested in running, and soon she was running alongside her father each morning. Day after day, week after week, month after month, the father-daughter team ran through the neighborhood.

To encourage others to treat epileptics like normal people, Patty decided to run from Orange County to San Francisco, a distance of four hundred miles, at the end of her freshman year of high school. That became her major goal. She had the faith and decided that she would pay the price and succeed.

Patty made an investment of one year in tough training. And she made the run. By that time, she spent nearly an hour every day in training, getting herself in top physical condition. She then expanded her goal. "At the end of my sophomore year," she said, "I'll run from Orange County to Portland, Oregon [a distance of more than one thousand miles]."

By this time, thousands of people were inspired by her. A book entitled *Run, Patty, Run* was published. At the end of her sophomore year, she was ready to try for Portland, Oregon. On the day the event was to begin, Patty's high school classmates stretched a big paper banner across the street. The high school band played. I offered a prayer for her success, and I took a medallion from around my neck to place around hers. On the back of the medallion were the words of the Possibility Thinker's creed: "When faced with a mountain,

I will not quit. I will keep on striving until I climb over, find a path through, tunnel underneath, or simply stay and turn the mountain into a gold mine, with God's help."

Then Patty started running, ripping through the paper banner and leaving it shredded behind her. But problems began to attack her. Patty fractured her foot, but she knew there were thousands of people who were expecting her to run and complete the trip. "Doctor," she said, "if you wrap it very tightly, don't you think I could keep running?" She tightly bound her foot and kept running.

Thirteen hundred miles brought her to the outskirts of Portland, Oregon. The governor of the state got his running suit on, joined her, and ran the last mile with her! The entire town was out to greet her. What a welcome she got! She had endured the pain. She had paid the price. She had survived and had succeeded. She had learned that faith has incredible mountain-moving power—if you will hang on and not give up when you seem to be surrounded by impossibilities.

Faith begins when you
believe in the ideas that
God sends you

*If you
believe it,
you can
achieve it*

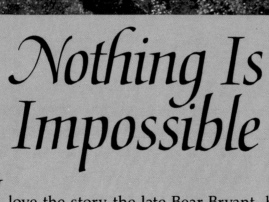

# Nothing Is Impossible

*I* love the story the late Bear Bryant, head football coach at the University of Alabama for many years, told me once. Years ago, when he was coach at Texas A&M, his team was scheduled to play SMU in one of the big bowl games. He said, "All of the newspapers said that my team was going to get swamped. These

were the words they used: *slaughtered, swamped, driven into the ground*. There was no way I could keep my boys from reading those negative forecasts. So I went to bed the night before the game, and suddenly I remembered all that the reporters and sportscasters were saying: 'Bear

Bryant of Texas A&M is going to get beaten by three or four touchdowns.' Others were saying five touchdowns. All of these extremely negative words were in my mind as I fell asleep. I woke up early in the morning. I looked at the clock and it was one o'clock.

"And I was petrified. We were going to get slaughtered. That was the forecast."

Then he said, "I remembered that Bible verse: 'If you have faith as a grain of mustard seed, you will say to this mountain, "Move from here to there," and it will move; and nothing shall be impossible unto you' [Matt. 17:20 KJV]. I got up, called my coaches, and said, 'I want you to have all the players in the locker room in thirty minutes.' I pulled my

pants on, put some shoes and a sweater on. I got in the car and started it. The two headlights pierced the blackness of the night. At 1:30 A.M. there wasn't a car on the road. I swung into the parking lot, went into the deserted locker room, paced, and waited. Other car lights started appearing, one lonely car after another. The players came staggering in. A couple of them were still in their pajamas and bathrobes.

"I said to them, 'Did you hear the news? Have you heard what they're predicting? They say we're going to get slaughtered. Beaten by four, five, or six touchdowns. You all heard it. O.K. I want to tell you something. Jesus said, "If you have faith as a grain of mustard seed— a little mustard seed—you can say to the mountain, Move! And it will move. And nothing will be impossible to you." Now go home to bed.'"

I asked him, "How did you do?"

He said, "Dr. Schuller, we lost. But by only three points. We lost the game, but boy, we saved our pride!"

The me I see . . .
is the me I'll be!

# He Walks with Me

*I* was in Korea to speak at the church of my friend Sundo Kim when I heard that my daughter Carol had been seriously injured in a motorcycle accident. My wife and I flew to Carol's bedside in Sioux City, Iowa. I was shocked. Carol's body was bruised, broken, and disfigured. But her spirits were whole and healthy.

On the long trip back, I had searched for my first words to her. But she spoke first: "I know why it happened, Dad. God wants to use me to help others who have been hurt."

It was this spirit, this positive attitude, that carried her through seven months of hospital-ization and helped Carol make the transition

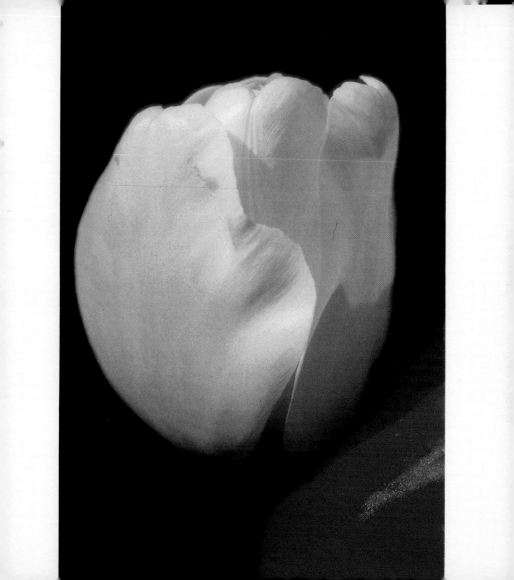

from hospital patient to "handicapped" member of a family and school. It helped her feel normal and whole again. She refused to allow the inconvenience of an artificial limb to keep her from pursuing the active life she loved.

The summer after her accident, she shocked me by saying, "Dad, I'm going to sign up for softball again this year."

"That's great!" I responded, not wanting to discourage her. "But how do you expect to play ball if you can't run?" With flashing eyes she snapped back at me, "When you hit home runs, you don't have to run."

My daughter is tough. She's a survivor. She has had six surgeries since that first amputation. Today she is skiing and has a gold medal in the qualifying races that admitted her to that elite corps of skiers participating in the National Ski Championships!

Last summer my family and I were on a cruise. It is customary on the last night of the cruise to have a talent show. Carol surprised us by saying, "I'm going to be in the talent show tonight."

Now Carol doesn't sing, and of course she doesn't dance. So, naturally, I was curious as to what she would do. Carol's not in the least ashamed to be seen in shorts or swimming attire, but she is very conscious of the fact that people wonder what happened to her.

On the night of the talent show, my wife and I sat with six hundred other people. Carol came on stage wearing a full length dress. She looked beautiful. She walked up to the microphone and said, "I thought this would be a

good chance for me to give what I think I owe you all: an explanation. I know you have been looking at me all week and wondering about my fake leg. I was in a motorcycle accident and I almost died."

She paused a moment. "If I have one talent," she continued, "it is this: I can tell you that during that time my faith became very real to me. I look at you girls who walk without a limp, and I wish I could walk that way. I can't, but this is what I've learned: It's not how you walk that counts, but who walks with you."

And then she sang

> And He walks with me,
> And He talks with me
> And He tells me I am His own,
> And the joy we share
>   in our time of prayer
> None other has ever known.*

You can do anything you think
you can, but you can't do it alone

*God should be a resource in the struggle, not a way around it.*

# The Faith That Can Move Your Mountain

Faith is indeed the greatest miracle-working power imaginable. Faith never fails a person; we fail when we give up on our faith. However, if we cut out any one of the five phases of mountain-moving faith, we will be disappointed with the ultimate results.

## The Nesting Phase

The first phase of faith is when an idea drops into your mind. For too many people, an idea passes through their mind without being taken seriously. Every human being has virtually equal creative potential. But most people have never been told they are creative and they have never tried to be. To make sure you develop mountain-moving faith, build a positive self-image. Hold a mental picture, and it will turn into a physical reality. Hold a negative picture, and negative results will happen. Draw now a positive picture of yourself, believe in your ideas, and faith will survive phase one.

### The Testing Phase

Faith's second phase is when ideas are tested by asking the questions that arise out of your own value system. How do you test the ideas that come into your mind? I test mine by this universal principle: *Will my faith, acted upon and firmly embraced, cause my life and my activity to be an inspiration to somebody else to become a better person or to achieve more in his life?*

### The Investing Phase

The third phase of faith is the point at which you make a public commitment. You commit time, money, energy, and—possibly the most valuable products of all—pride and prestige. At this point, many people find their faith faltering. If, by an act of will and prayer, you determine that you will make the public commitment, the odds are overwhelming that you can succeed.

### The Arresting Phase

In the fourth phase of faith, problems attack you. Troubles block you. You begin to think you've bitten off more than you can chew. The arresting phase of faith is God's way of testing us before the final victory. He wants to make sure: Are we really depending on Him? Will we really be grateful if we make it? Can He trust us with success? Don't trust the clouds—trust the sunshine. Trust in your hopes—never trust in your hurts. And you will move on eventually, effectively, inspiringly to faith's final phase.

## The Cresting Phase

Yes, the crowning phase of faith is the cresting phase. The mountaintop is scaled! Success finally is achieved! A habit is broken. The money starts flowing your way. The bones are healed. You walk back into the sunshine. A broken relationship is healed. The emptiness and loneliness of life is filled with a new friend and loved one. A job opportunity comes your way.

Those who keep on keeping on ultimately survive successfully and, in the process, are an incredible inspiration to others to keep bravely fighting their battles, too. God created you to be somebody who could be an inspiration to many people. Open your mind to receive possibility thoughts and be prepared to trust in them through the testing phase, the investing phase, the arresting phase. Never abandon the dream until you have reached the cresting phase!

Dream big, work hard,
and share your success

# Praying for Life

*I* remember the day when I received the telephone call that an elder of my church, Stanley Reimer, had had a twenty-two minute cardiac arrest. Obviously that was a considerable amount of time during which oxygen was not reaching his brain.

He was in what was called a "death coma." Although his body was breathing on its own, there was no other sign of life. The neurosurgeon told Stan's wife that there was no hope: "If he keeps breathing, he'll be a vegetable all of his life. He'll never close his eyes.

They'll be open in a death stare exactly as you see him now."

As soon as I heard the news, I rushed to the hospital, praying all the way, "God, what will I say to him? What will I say to his wife?"

I remembered that, in theological seminary, the professors had taught us: "Some day, as a pastor, you may talk to someone in a death

coma. When that happens, only think *life*, only talk *life*, only believe *life*. The patient may lack the power to indicate that he is hearing you, but his mind may be getting your messages. So you must not place a negative thought in his mind."

With that recollection I went into the intensive care unit where Stan was lying. Billie, his

wife, was standing at the bedside, tears streaming down her face. Stanley, my once-outgoing friend, could not move. From all practical appearances, he was dead. His eyes were wide open but indicated no life or responsiveness whatever.

I put my arm around Billie and prayed with her. Then I took hold of Stanley's hand and I said softly, my lips close to his ear, "Stanley, I know you cannot talk. I know you cannot respond to me. But I know that you can hear me. I am your pastor. This is Reverend Robert Schuller. I've just come from the church, where everyone is praying for you. And Stanley, I've got good news for you. Even though you've had a bad heart attack and are in a coma, you are going to recover. You are going to live. It's going to be a long battle. It's going to be hard and tough. But you are going to make it, Stanley!"

At that point, I had one of the most moving experiences of my life. Suddenly a tear rolled out of his staring eye! He understood! No smile; no quiver of a lip; but a tear rolled out of his eye. The doctor was shocked. Billie was shocked. One year later Stanley was able to speak full sentences. He was able to hear. His faculties were becoming normal. Today he walks and talks and laughs and is alive!

In the darkest times, simply remind yourself that faith can move any mountain.

*Faith is dead to doubt . . .*
*dumb to discouragement . . .*
*blind to impossibilities*